BOSS MY LIFE

CONTENTS

21
FOOD & CULTURE
Cinco De Mayo Fav

Editor's Note

BOSS MY LIFE MAGAZINE

We'll never stop providing the best content related to positive living in a magazine. It is my commitment and the entire Boss My Life Magazine team to always provide the latest and most substantive content on the local and international scene that display positivity and inspiration in life, love, fashion, entertainment, business, etc. because we believe our readers deserve the best.

Jacqueline Johnson

Editor-in-Chief

In this issue, let's have fun discovering, embracing and indulging in the joys that come with the summer season. Summer represents a shift in life's seasons and for many it's the epitome of an awakening on all fronts.

Tranquil HOT SPOTS

FEATURED DESTINATION

Dillon Beach Resort
California

Comfortable Stay

West Coast inspired Dillon Beach Resort is nestled between rustic ranches, rolling agrarian hillsides and perched upon the unparalleled beauty of the Northern Californian Pacific coast. Blink and you'll miss the turn-off for Dillon Beach in the quaint town of Tomales, Marin County's northernmost town. Dillon Beach has been Marin County's hidden gem for far too long. Come on out and enjoy this seaside village, explore the sand dunes, admire the tidepools and soak up the beach in all its splendor.

Day-trippers, weekenders and locals alike enjoy the expansive, dog-friendly privately owned beach. The perfect escape, only 30 minutes from the 101 in Petaluma, Dillon Beach feels worlds away.

Dillon Beach Resort sits on 55-coastal acres on the Marin-Sonoma County Line, between the mouth of Tomales and the entrance to Bodega Bay. Views of the magnificent Point Reyes Peninsula can be enjoyed from any vantage point on the property.

SURROUNDING COMFORTS

In additon to the beautiful tiny home styled living quarters, Dillon Beach Resort has a special well kept secret with its own local dining/store called, "Coastal Kitchen".

Coastal Kitchen

Inspired by farm & sea, Dillon Beach Coastal Kitchen highlights and celebrates local & seasonal cuisine. The Coastal Kitchen is an advocate for our local food shed, thoughtfully sourcing proteins, produce and products often directly from farmers, ranchers, foragers, and fishermen almost exclusively from Northern California. Our seasonally driven menu highlights the ingredients sourced from Marin and Sonoma Counties.

Boss Body
HEALTH &
Wellness

LOVE YOUR BODY

Healthy lifestyle is not about diets, weight loss, and every other series of words that bring fear and anxiety to men and women all over this word. Before you ever get to weight loss or a buff physique (for the fellas), a healthy lifestyle begins with your personal perception of body positivity.

Instead of focusing on that perfect body, simply try to create and maintain new healthy goals for yourself. Detoxing the body is first, eating healthier is second, and consistent physical activity is the third thing on that list.

Boss Body
HEALTH &
Wellness

When you hear physical activity it can be very traumatic, especially for those who are out of shape and haven't really been very active in a while. However I want you to breathe and let's remove that traumatic block.

Doing consistent physical activity doesn't mean hitting the gym everyday working on all the machines and running as fast as you can on the treadmill. It just means "get up everyday and move"!

Activities as simple as walking around the block of your home, going to the botanical gardens and walking around looking at and smelling all the different flowers, or just picking up the trash in your yard. All of these activities get you moving, therefore get a healthy circulation of blood flowing through your body.Not to mention it will get you outside your home and in some fresh air and sunlight. These things are important both for your physical and mental health.

If you start with these simple baby steps of physical activity and be consistent for at least a month (or until you feel comfortable) then move on to at least one activity more strenuous like a longer walk, or jump rope, steps, sit ups, set time on the treadmill, light weights, etc. Once you consistently do that activity in addition to the baby steps you've incorporated into your daily routine, when you're ready add another more strenuous activity. Your progress may not be as quick as others, but you'll be happier, healthier, and you'll feel better.

SUMMER
FASHIONS

By: Mikel Kindell

en it comes to fashion everyone is
ays checking the "trends" but
nestly true fashion is about displaying
ir individual style and personality
apologetically. Wearing whatever you
oose to wear regardless of the "likes"
compliments of others is true fashion
edom.

s summer focus on displaying
twardly the joy and excitement you're
ticipating in your life. Let the colors
u wear and the styles you choose truly
lect the "you" that you want the world
see. If you're the comfortable, chill
d of person that can be translated in a
ple tee with your favorite saying,
ote, or life mantra printed on it.

ou're a fun loving, free and fancy
da person then bright colors,
k/crop tops with comfortable bottoms
a colorful flowy sundress may be for
u. It honestly isn't about what you
ar, it's how confidently/comfortably
u wear it.

DRESSING LOUD

Next, for my plus size ladies and gentleman.
Summer time is a time of letting your hair down.
It can be hard to be confident and free especially
when you don't have a great body image outlook.
I want to challenge you to wear clothes that fit
snugly to your body and avoid the loose,
comfortable normal frumpy wear that we tell
ourselves all full-figured people should wear.

It's time to live in the joy of today. I will admit
that black is very slimming however in the
summer months let's remember that darker
colors retain more heat. If you're going to stick to
your dark

VIBRANT
OUTFITS

BREAK OUT OF
YOUR NORMAL

color scheme then at least add vibrant bright colors in the form of accessories like belts, light scarves, sunglasses, beach bags/purses, shoes, etc. It's also important to be careful of the materials your clothing is made of. For summertime try to stick with thin materials such as cottons, polyester blends, and sheer fabrics. These materials will be more comfortable on your skin. And for plus size folks especially ladies who just don't like their arms. Use big sleeves to hide flabby arms. Avoid patterns as solid colors help to hide fupas and unwanted tummy fat.

Congratulations
to our
GRADUATES!

Best wishes for
a bright future!

THE GATEWAY TO INDEPENDENCE

Written By: Jackie Johnson

The last five years my family and I have been blessed to call the small community of Boyle, Heights our home. Many people have asked us through the years how has life been for us as Black Americans living in a predominantly Hispanic/Latin X community and my response hasn't changed, "It's been enlightening, adventurous, as well as welcoming."

At the root of these experiences has been our connection to my children's high school. Felicitas & Gonzalo Mendez High School has been a core part of our lives and has given us stronger ties of community and comfortability.

After re-locating our family from Columbus, OH in 2018 we had no idea what to expect from our new life in Los Angeles, CA. We followed the leading of the

Photo from: INSTAGRAM | @leadership.mhs

ly Spirit to greater pastures. Therefore walking by faith and not by sight we were led to this amazing community that has nurtured and supported our community ties and personal journeys.

Mendez High School thrives and is continually growing and expanding yearly under the phenomenal leadership of the Principal, Mr. Mario Bautista who truly has a love, passion and genuine concern for the students, staff, and community as a whole.. His personal yet professional interactions are powerful, impactful, and inspirational to the community he not only serves and represents, but is a part of.

There are so many teachers and staff members at Mendez High School that go above and beyond to support and encourage the students to do and be greater, that also add to the overall environment of the school which promotes family and community. It's the greatest reason that I personally love and value this school. Even as a parent with three children who graduated from this phenomenal establishment, I have formed life-long professional and personal relationships and community ties through my involvement and volunteer work with the school. With the last of my children completing his high school experience here. I personally want to thank Principal Bautista and the entire staff for their service, support, and commitment to the success of my children & all others before and after them.

Photo from: INSTAGRAM | @leadership.mhs

Principal: Mario Bautista

The last year of high school so often can be a sad one because students are leaving behind the lives they've known and grown comfortable with for the last four years of their lives; from the supportive community of teachers, coaches, counselors, family, and friends to the brotherhood/sisterhood that's formed through the bonds of clubs, extracurricular actives, and sports teams. However, Senior year of High School represents so much more. It represents a time of transition, adventure, and maturity.

There are traditional high school events that are designed to celebrate both the accomplishments of students through their dedication, consistency, and hard-work as well as their chosen pathways towards the life they've been dreaming about.

The two most popular celebratory events are "PROM" and "Graduation Commencement". I had the privilege of seeing the joy and traditions being displayed live and in living color through my graduating senior. I can't tell you the joy, beauty, and hope for the future it brought to my heart, mind and spirit.

HELLO *prom*

Mendez High School celebrated their 2023 Prom Celebration at the beautiful LA River Gardens on May 19th. This beautiful location gave the Mendez Seniors a beautiful night of enchantment.

-Photo from Instagram | @leadership.mhs

Prom Royalty

Photographer: Brenda Janairo

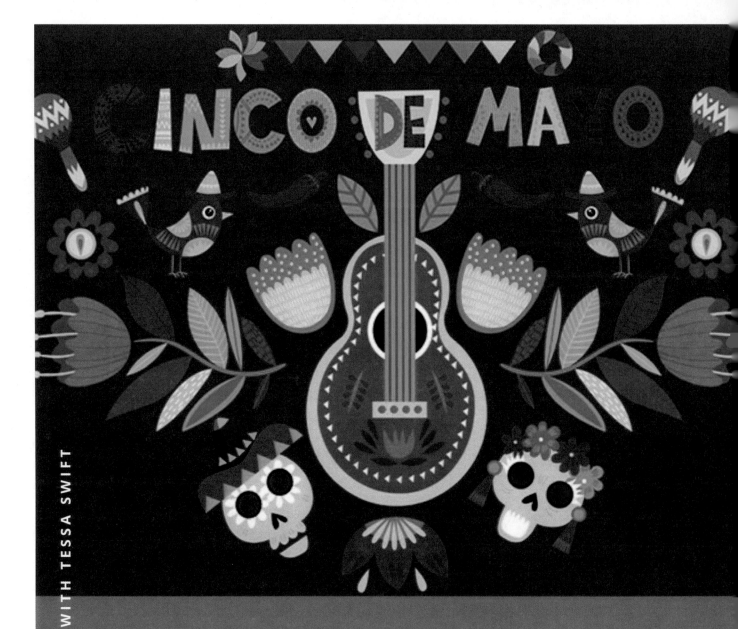

FOOD & CULTURE

CARNE CON PAPAS IN VERDE SAUCE
TESSA SWIFT

Writer Tessa Swift

For Cinco de Mayo this year I made one of my boyfriend's easy, yet super delicious Mexican favorites, carne con papas in a verde sauce. This beef and potato dish is sure to be a family favorite and is simple enough to incorporate into your weeknight dinner rotation. The verde sauce is rich and flavorful with just the right amount of kick from the chiles, and the beef slow simmered is tender and a perfect compliment with the buttery potatoes. Served with tortillas and queso fresco this dish is absolutely too delicious not to share!

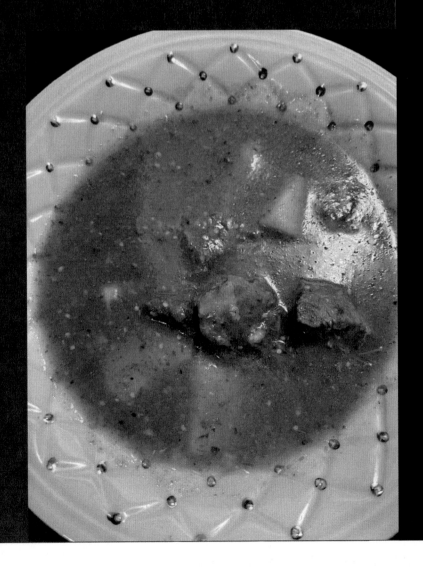

To make this dish you will need the following ingredients:

- 2lbs beef (I chose stewing beef chunks)
- 3 russet potatoes diced into 1 ½ cubes (place your diced potatoes in cold wat to avoid oxidation)
- 1 ½lbs tomatillos
- ¼ white onions
- 4 chile serrano
- 1 whole bunch cilantro
- 2tsp vegetable oil
- 1 ½ tsp salt
- ½ tsp black pepper
- 1tsp oregano
- ½ tsp garlic powder
- ½ tsp cumin
- 2tbs Knorr Caldo de Pollo (chicken bouillon seasoning)
- 9 cups water

DIRECTIONS

1. Rinse all your vegetables and in a large pot combine 4cups of water, all of your tomatillos, chiles, and onion. Boil the vegetables until the tomatillos have changed from a bright to darker green.
2. While your tomatillos and chilies are boiling, season your beef with salt and pepper. Add the oil to a large pot and brown your beef. I like to complete brown my beef on all sides. Don't worry about if your meat gets tough you will be stewing it shortly and it will be completely tender when done.
3. While your beef is browning, drain your now dark green tomatillos, along with the chilies and onion and place into a blender with the remainder of the seasonings along with the whole bunch of cilantro and 2cups of water, and blend until smooth.
4. Pour your now delicious and spicy verde sauce into the pot with the beef and the remaining 3 cups of water, and place your pot on high heat.
5. Once the pot comes to a boil, cover and lower the stove to medium-low and simmer for 40 mins.
6. After 40 mins add your diced potatoes and simmer for an additional 20 mins or until potatoes are fork tender.
7. Serve with warm corn tortillas and fresh queso fresco. Enjoy!

THERAPY HOUR

NAVIGATING TRANSITIONS AS A PARENT

JENNIFER A. MARION, MA MFTA

WWW.SHESEVOLVINGTHECOLLECTIVE.COM

I'm blessed to be a mother of six children. I can remember the birth of each one of my babies besides my stepson. Becoming a parent is a joyful, exciting, and fulfilling experience. It's profound and unexplainable. The family life cycle includes transition points families experience to identify change and/or potential stressors in the family.

As parents, we navigate through many transitions throughout our children's lives. We struggle with changes as adults transitioning into parenthood. Our children transition into childcare and school, adolescence, through committed friend relationships and relationships with a significant other, getting a job and a driver's license, and leaving the home to start a career or attend college.

I have found myself as a mother struggling with the transition of my oldest daughter. Our children are a blessing. However, they grow up quickly! My sons graduated from high school in prior years. My oldest son is in the United States Army stationed at Fort Bragg, North Carolina.
He's married and working hard in his career to prepare to start his family. My other son decided to take a career in the

auto industry and is now transitioning to the United States Air Force within the next few months. I'm so godly proud of both my sons for their hard work, dedication, and determination to succeed.

May 5-7, 2023, I spent my time supporting my daughter at her last AHSAA State Championship for track and field. My daughter has qualified for the State Championship for track and field for the past three years. This particular year is different since it's her last track season as a high school student. My daughter is a Senior at this high school heading to college in the Fall of 2023. I experienced mixed emotions concerning her upcoming graduation and transition to college. My daughter isn't my first child leaving the home, but she is my first girl leaving home.

There are parents all over the county sharing mixed emotions concerning their children preparing to leave home for the first time. As parents, we focus on ensuring our children are making the right decision. We might struggle with empty nesting, grief or loss, confusion, and mixed emotions. I had to learn to embrace the new role transitioning from a parent to a personal life coach. I'm not leaving my child or letting her go. My role in her life is shifting. I will still be in the background aiding as needed. I will no longer have control of the reins. Here are a few strategies I want to provide you with to help with the transition.

Parents, we must stop and give ourselves pats on the back. We did it! Bask in that accomplishment alongside your child. As a parent, you must know it's perfectly fine and/or normal for you to have moments of sadness. A child leaving the home is a huge transition. One day the child is an infant and you blink and they're graduating high school. Having feelings of sadness is normal. Trust yourself and/or your significant other that the hard work it took to instill life lessons and teachings to them will prepare them. I know you have done enough. If difficulties arise with you not being able to release sadness and it transitions to depression, seek a mental health provider. There are resources available for parents to find relief from mental and emotional concerns by adding another layer of support. Find support systems or support groups related to what you need.

Stay calm and focused. Give yourself grace that your child has made the right decision and it will pay off in the future. Give your child credit. Sometimes we focus on negative things more than considering the positive things. Take a step back and realize your child must become an adult in this society and you have prepared them to prosper.

Take moments through the transition to schedule self-care time to relax. Identify new personal goals or career goals and needs for yourself. What will change for you with your child leaving? How do you make the necessary adjustments? Use your time wisely to reconnect to people, places, things, or hobbies. Learn how to rest and relax. Create a safe place for yourself that is therapeutic and will assist you with handling the range of emotions you might experience when your child leaves home.

I'Encourage them through affirmation they will succeed. They are entering into a world of adulthood. Affirm them in knowing they can make decisions on their own and care for themselves. Provide your child with assurance, you will always be their advocate. You don't have to let go of your child. Stay connected. Give them space to become independent, brave, and full of strength. Even if they have weak moments throughout their future endeavors, God's grace is sufficient that in our weaknesses, He makes us strong. Give them the ability to step out on their own.

Take negative thoughts captive immediately. Your thoughts influence your feelings/emotions, and your feelings/emotions influence your behaviors. Negative thoughts will always incite negative feelings/emotions and behaviors. If your child hasn't called you back in hours, it doesn't mean anything is wrong. They could have left their phone in the dorms while they were studying in the library. Use Philippians 4:8 to meditate on if you struggle with negative thoughts. Getting your thoughts in control will decrease your chances of overreacting.

Pray always. Prayer is direct communication between you and God. Make time to devote yourself to God through prayer and reading His word. The word of God has scriptures based on everything in life we can deal with. Find scriptures that align to your life and use them. Use the scriptures to pray for your child. Make sure to pray for yourself, your health, and well-being.

We're on this journey together. Your child is prepared because you have provided them support, encouragement, wisdom, life lessons, set boundaries, and trusted God to watch over them. You have worked hard for this milestone. Now it's time to watch your child grow.

KAY G BEAUTY

BEAUTY-FULL

KAY KINDELL

MY

TOP MAKEUP BRAND FAVS

BEAUTY IS MORE THAN SKIN DEEP

Kg

PERSONAL FAVS

Foundation

**FIT ME
By Mabeline**

**FENTY
BEAUTY**

PERSONAL FAVS

Eye Shadow

JUVIA'S PLACE

Setting Spray

MILANI

PERSONAL FAVS

Lips

KAYLA GIRLS LIP GLOSS

JUVIA'S PLACE LIPSTICK

BEAUTY IS MORE
THAN SKIN DEEP

Kay Kay Kindell

Culture and our environments have taught us that beauty is the "Greater" thing. There are even studies that show that people who are more attractive do better in every area of life; from careers, love & marriage, and even money. And while I agree to an extend that this is true. I think the reason I beleive it to be true is different from most of those studies.

The truth is that beauty breeds "confidence". Confidence gives a person a better chance of being noticed in almost every arena. Who doesn't take notice when an unusually beautiful woman or extremely handsome man walks into the room?

However, how many times has that person's beauty been overshadowed by their nasty attitude, cocky disposition and overall standoffish demeanor? I can say from my own personal experiences that the answer is too many times. Which is why it's important to work on your inner beauty just as much as your outer beauty.

Practice being kind to others, giving another woman a compliment (men telling another man you respect something about him), etc. No matter how beautiful you are on the outside, your true beauty doesn't reveal itself until you interact with those around you, from strangers, co-workers, friends, family, and loved-ones: it all matters.

ALONE
NOT
LONELY

In a world where relationships and power couples are glorified, society has left little room for positive singles representation. The general consensus for most people is that being alone (without a mate/spouse) means that a person is somehow lacking somewhere and therefore the result is that they don't have a suitable partner. However, this is far from the truth. There is a time and season for singleness.

Singleness is not a place of embarrassment, lack, or not being good enough. Singleness is a designated time of self discovery, adventure and preparation. It's designed for individuals to take time to love and appreciate themselves as well as discovering their purpose, desires hopes and dreams for life. It is extremely important for individuals to fully embrace and experience this period of time before a person ever enters into a romantic relationship with another person.

Sadly, most people either experience a small fraction of this single freedom or others don't experience it all. This disservice creates problematic pathways within a person's life that makes relationships almost inevitable for failure for a variety of reasons. The root of many breakups, separations, and divorces can be traced back to this very issue at its root. People who have never embraced seasons of singleness properly in their lives may experience seemingly successful relationships and even marriages but only for an extended period of time. Ultimately it will cause other minor issues that seem big and unsolvable within the relationship. The individuals most often don't recognize the true issue because they focus on the minor issues which become their reasons or excuses to call it quits, stop trying, or move on to someone else (believing it will solve their problem of unhappiness or dissatisfaction).

However unless individuals come to a place of understanding within their relationship and they have a partner that is patient enough and willing to help them during their process the relationship is doomed to fail. Which is why there are so many people entering into serious relationships without dealing with the issues and dysfunctional behavior they previously inherited.

This is why even after failed relationships happen, individuals should take adequate time away from relationships for healing and self-discovery or re-discovery. Although this can begin as a time of discouragement, disappointment, and disheartening it will evolve into a time of freedom, adventure, discovery, revelation, lasting inner peace & joy.

Many people discover/re-discover their self-worth and learn to see and love themselves (their true selves). They embark on journey's never taken before, dream dreams they didn't believe they had the right to dream before, and they go after goals they were too afraid or distracted to achieve before, and some people just rest from a life of taking care of everyone se but themselves. In a nut shell, singleness is a time of awakening.

This time of awakening that's meant to be lived both quietly and out loud. There's a joy in becoming accountable to only yourself and God as opposed to considering the thoughts, feelings, and well-being of everyone around you and making decisions that can be uncomfortable and/or unpleasant to your own feelings because it's what's best for the unit or "whole".

When some people fully embrace their singleness they experience a freedom, joy, peace, and environment of fun they may have never really known before. Because of this new experience many people can find comfort and a sense of security in this place of solitude, so much so that they reject the desire or possibility of trying love, relationships, and marriage ever again.

However I want to encourage those of you who may be here in the solitude part of your journey not to close your heart to love. God said, "It's not good for man to be alone" so he made Adam a help meet (a partner and a companion), you were created to be someone's partner. I want to remind you that solitude is a great place to be until God sends your partner to you, then you have to be open and aware enough to make that decision/choice based on your new wisdom and clarity that your season of singleness helped you to develop. Alone doesn't have to mean, LONELY!

Coming Soon!

MK EXPERIENCE

The. Genesis

MK·60·6 | Fe | МЭКΙ | 1991

MK EXPERIENCE

 @themkexpo

PS MUSIC GROUP

BOSS

Devotions

DEVOTIONS FROM THE BOOK:

Boss Pearls

JUNE 1-15

WEEK 1: "TRUE SELF"

"Environment can help mold you...
But when you meet God; it's HE that
births you into your TRUE SELF"
St. John 15:19

WEEK 2: "HUSTLE"

"When you're chasing your dream,
building your foundation, or
protecting your empire, you will get
tired, you will even feel lonely, but
have FAITH and keep HUSTLING"
Proverbs 29:18

JUNE 16-30

WEEK 3: "GREATNESS"

"One of the greatest enemies of
entrepreneurship is "Mediocrity". So, yo
must remind yourself daily that God has
destined you to be Great, no matter who
doesn't like it."
Matthew 5:13

WEEK 4: "FIGHT"

"Sometimes the enemy you'll have to fac
isn't those around you: it will be the bea
that lives within you. Fighting against
every place that threatens who you real
are."
Numbers 10:9

JLY 1-16

WEEK 1: "LITTLE STEPS"

"You may think that the steps you're taking today are small; but it's those little steps that will establish you as a GIANT tomorrow"
Matthew 14:29

WEEK 2: "SUCCESS"

"It's not about becoming an overnight success. It's about the step by step choices you make to lay a firm foundation, strong enough to handle the weight of your empire"
I Corinthians 3:14

JULY 17-31

WEEK 3: "HONOR"

"Only those that are HONORABLE, know how to give HONOR to others."
Romans 12:10

WEEK 4: "DREAM"

"If you build it... Success will come, but never allow comfortability to hinder you from continually dreaming!"
Acts 2:17

AUGUST 1-16

WEEK 1: "REAL BOSSES"

"A real boss is never threatened by the success of others, They CELEBRATE it!"
Philippians 2:3

WEEK 2: "BELIEVE"

"Life will challenge who you think you are...God will remind you who you really are... BUT it's your actions that will show the world who you chose to believe!"
Jeremiah 1:5

AUGUST 17-31

WEEK 3: "THINK & LIVE"

"Think like an entrepreneur and eventually you'll get to live like a BOSS."
Romans 12:2

WEEK 4: "EVOLVE"

"Be sure that who you are now, is able to keep up with who you're becoming. Som will call it switching up, but real people will see it for what it is: which is your evolution"
Philippians 3:14

SEPTEMBER 1-15

WEEK 1: "GO GET IT"

Don't allow anyone or anything to keep you from reaching new heights and deeper depths. If God said it, that's all you need to know; don't leave anything on the table. Go get it ALL"
Romans 8:31

WEEK 2: "PROCRASTINATION"

Don't allow procrastination to kill the greatness within you, or you'll end up like so many others who've taken their dreams and potential to the grave!"
Ecclesiastes 9:10

SEPTEMBER 16-30

WEEK 3: "HELP OR HURT"

"Don't confuse the people that God sends into your life to help you, with those who sneak in your life to hurt you."
I Thessalonians 5:12

WEEK 4: "PROTECT THE CIRCLE"

"The circle are people that believed in and supported you from the moment they entered your life until now. Appreciate them and protect those relationships because a Boss is only as good as their support team"
Ruth 1:16

MY SISTAH & ME

RELATIONSHIP STATUS

WATSON & JOHNSON

FAMILY TIES: Eric & Latoria Curry

Redesign Your L8ve & Marriage in Forgiveness

I remember like it was yesterday when I was a seven year old child. I am my mother's only child, therefore my room was always full of beautiful dolls (both boy and girl dolls). My tv channel stayed on happy, family type shows, and because of this all I did was fantasize about being a mother and a wife. It's what I was seeing around me; family and love. In the early years of growing up all I knew where beautiful, happy, smiling, relationships among those that babysit me, my uncles & aunts, older cousins, friends of the family, etc. Everywhere I looked, it was obvious that "Love" was the gaol.

So I began studying love and I was proud to declare that I wanted to be a wife and mother. My environment had been saturated with love and marriage and I was soaking it all up. In the 80's & 90's it seemed like everyone was in love. They all seemed to be so happy. I used to watch my uncle (my mother's baby brother- God rest his soul), he always kept me with him everywhere he went. He was my first example that showed me how a man was supposed to treat a woman he loved.

During this time my uncle was around 24yrs old. He had a beautiful girlfriend who later became his first child's mother. They gave me such a beautiful preview of what real, happy, fun, excited, sexy, and faithful love looks like. I was stuck with that image of love for so long. I loved to be around my uncle and his girlfriend

He always played beautiful R&B love songs like Keith Sweat, Hi-Five, Gerald Levert, The Isley Brothers, and others. I can on and on because these songs along with my uncle and his girlfriend's example influenced my perception of love. I thought that love, marriage, and family was all we were supposed to be and have. I had no desire to be anything more.

As I journeyed through life, my desire was to always study and choose the "frog I would kiss and turn into the prince," but what I found out as I became wiser is that everybody was raised and taught about love differently . Each household had their own concept of their personal limitations as well as their own definition that molded what they believed love to be or not to be, and at this point I was trying to live out my life based on the things I had seen growing up. I started dating at the very young age of thirteen, I know most people will read this and think how weird that sounds, but it's true. I needed guidance and proper training because it was in me to walk in love, not fall in love and get stuck like so many youth do by being so young with limited understanding about love and relationships.

I didn't understand that all romantic relationships weren't the same. There was a difference between real love and what people saw on television and in their individual environments.

I thought all relationships operated the same way, but oh how wrong I was! I saw myself as a teenager experiencing heartbreak. I know what heartache feels like. It's a pain that I wish on no one. At thirteen years old I felt what a lot of people are feeling today.

My whole perspective of relationships changed. I was just like so many grown and young people in the world after being hurt, saying I would never get married. My mind was made up that allmen were dirty liars. My heart grew bitter because I had never seen the pain that came with love. As a teen at the ages of sixteen and seventeen I was operating from a one sided mindset, believing that no one could be trusted except GOD!

God softened my heart by reminding me of the where my viewpoint about love came from. I heard God tell me to, "Go create the love you desire." Therefore when I was eighteen I felt I was ready for whatever. When I came across women or men who had the love or companionship I dreamed of having since I was seven years old and I saw them abuse it in any way, I would instantly become angry and cut them off and some I never talked to again, all because I felt that if you didn't care how you represented the people who love you then I knew I couldn't trust you to care about me and you'd never be a loyal friend to me.

God didn't want me to judge the pureness of what he showed me at seven years old. He was showing me the kind of love he ordained for me to receive but I had misunderstood and began trying to obtain it in my own strength and intellect. So, I tries it again, this time I was much older and could study the definition of love and forgiveness.

I changed my mind and decided I wanted to get married after all. It took me seven years in a relationship with my husband before I said I do because I knew that once I was married, I'd be in it for the long haul. God started blessing me and my husband with friends who had long lasting, pure marriages. Through these encounters I learned that the true secret for a long, beautiful, happy marriage designed by God for us to have is, unconditional love and forgiveness.

Marriage is not for show and it's not a game. Marriage is a divine covenant, a promise, and a solemn oath. Just like God forgives us when we come to him broken, apologetic, and asking for his forgiveness; HE wants us to be the same way in dealing with our spouse.

Marriage is for those who beleive in the power of God. It's for those who believe that God is love and forgiveness. Marriage exposes if you're a truth teller or a liar. I do understand that some some marriages are not of God. However, I am speaking to those who believe that their marriage is the result of true love (which is rooted in God). Our creator will teach you to forgive like Him. He understands your human nature, which is why he uses patience and grace when showing us the way. God will also align your partner up, even when you both feel like throwing in the towel.

My hsuband and I both believed in the love of God and our love for each other. We are human just like you and when the worse came to attack our family, we made the same mistakes most people do and tried to live our lives without one another. We had given up on what we both had been investing in for over ten years. We had the same mindset.

Marriage is hard work but worth the results just like a great paying job often requires more effort than an entry-level position. Every time my husband and I attempted to move on, we really would realize how much we loved each other. We had to keep forgiving each other over and over again until we saw transformation in our lives. We both vowed that we would not give up.

We always explain to our children that we are relearning and developing our family on healthy and godly principals. My husband and I were taking test in the subject of family that we had never taken before. We were honest and transparent with our five children and asked for forgiveness countless times for the errors we performed before them. We were praying daily for God to fix all the wrong things in our lives so we could show our children a different way, the God way. We want married believers everywhere to understand that forgiveness stands in the center of God's love for us and in order to fulfill your vows, you will need the ability to forgive daily.

"Whatever the storm your facing, remember Jesus Christ is the director"

-Eric Curry

"The greatest human act is forgiveness"

-Latoria Curry

BOSS MONEY

IN OUR LAST ISSUE WE TALKED ABOUT THE
POWER OF BUDGETING. IN THIS ISSUE WE
WOULD LIKE TO DISCUSS SAVINGS!

EVERY PERSON SHOULD HAVE AT LEAST 3 SAVINGS ACCOUNTS

ACCOUNT #1- EMERGENCY SAVINGS

for those unplanned needs that can pop up out of the blue as well as
your cost of living for a year in case of UNFORESEEN loss of income!
(This should be at least 6x your monthly cost of living)

ACCOUNT #2- SHORT TERM GOALS

this can be traveling, or a physical item you're looking to purchase
like a car, boat, computer, etc.

ACCOUNT #3-LONG TERM GOALS & INVESTMENTS

this is to provide your own retirement $, business venture,
investment $

*Following these simple steps (weather $50/wk or
$50/month) helps to put you and your household in a better
financial position.* If you're not yet achieving these savings
goals, don't beat yourself up, just know it's time to start today
making new money habits!

THE GOOD SHEPHERD GOD IS

THE GOSPEL TRUTH

Written By:
Dr. Dorvetta Price

WHAT IS A GOOD SHEPHERD?

DR. DORVETTA PRICE

As shepherd of the sheep, He is the one who protects, guides, and nurtures His flock. The shepherd cares so much for his flock that he regards his life as equal to theirs. He is willing to lay down his life for them. The shepherd directs the flock of sheep to graze in the field, through the wilderness, back to shelter, Jesus does the same for believers. The bad shepherd (pharaoh) is filled with greed, they are selfish, think of only themselves and want to be served all the time. They think the sheep should take care of their every need. They're too good to take out trash or clean the house of God. They walk over & look over when there is work to be done, it's never their job because they carry the title of Pastor, Prophet, Apostle etc. A real parent takes care of their children. A child can't see to the needs of the parent. Somebody has to lead by example.

"AS CHRISTIANS
WHEN W
ACKNOWLEDGE THA
GOD IS ACTING A.
OUR SHEPHERD THER
ARE A FEW
PRINCIPLES WE CAN
BE SURE OF"

What should I feel from the shepherd of the house?

As Christians, when we acknowledge that God is acting as our shepherd there are a few principles we can be sure of.

1. God Cares-------
The Pastor(s) of the house should show signs of caring such as Jesus. This means the pastor goes out of his way to take care of the needs of the people. Kingdom pastors are waiters, they still clean bathrooms sweep floors, take out trash, do street ministry, deliverance sessions, alter work, pray for the people, visit the sick, and most of all they **SHOW UP READY TO WORK MINISTRY**!

The pastor should be the first in everything and ready to work. A leader shows others how to do. Pastor(s) if you are acting like a child you are not qualified to run the daycare. In other words, sit down, get out the way so God can raise up a pastor after His heart to run His daycare. It's time to grow up and get out of your feelings.

Shepherd if you are disobedient, a back-bitter, lazy etc. no one will respect you/ listen to you and some will even follow your patterns.

Shepherd you are to be an example ALL the time for the sake of the people. Learn to hold your tongue so God can work on your half. The sheep should never know your thoughts or opinion on matters. Stop being common with God's people. Church Pastors don't clean bathrooms,pray for the people, do street ministry, visit the sick etc., they expect to be waited on and served hand/foot neglecting the needs of the people. Preaching is not waiting on the people but showing them how you care for them so they will in return know how to care for each other and new converts.

"I am the good shepherd. The good shepherd lays down his life for the sheep." (John 10:11). As much as a shepherd looks after His flock, so does God look after us, His children. A shepherd protects his flock because he cares for his herd, his belongings. We belong to God and therefore we have value in His eyes. As written in John 10:11, a shepherd will lay "down his life for his sheep." That's exactly what Jesus did for us on the Cross. Jesus spoke in this fashion before dying on our behalf. This is all the more reason to cement our faith and believe.

2. God Provides-----

Dear Pastors, study the word! Stop giving a word from your opinion to the people but instead release "The Word" to the people of God. People will hear The Word before your words. Teach the people by being a example of how God provides. People learn by examples. Pastors be first to sacrifice; If you broke all the time something is wrong. And (1 Timothy 3:4-5) reads as follows, "One that ruleth well his own house, having his children in subjection with all gravity; (For if a man know not how to rule his own house, how shall he take care of the church of God?)"

Pastors/Shepherds you are always the first to be partakers of the sacrifice. What is she taking about? BILLS AT THE CHURCH! If the lead pastor is called to another assignment or dies, can you continue the work or will it die in your care because the people don't trust you to give?

Sometimes pastors have to carry the ministry financially until people trust you. People will only commit to what they believe in and they will just hang around to see how far you go."The Lord is my shepherd, I lack nothing. He makes me lie down in green pastures, he leads me beside quiet waters, he refreshes my soul. He guides me along the right paths for his name's sake." (Psalm 23:1-3)

A herd of animals may survive on their own in the wilderness, but a herd taken care of by a good shepherd is bound to live a more abundant life. The same applies to humanity when we strive to live our lives in tandem with God. Much like this psalm, God acts as our Shepherd by providing us those places of food and water. Extending outside of the animal metaphor, God provides us with shelter, money, and other resources. This is not to say that He will not allow for moments when we go without, but even in seasons where we lack specific resources, God is always providing what we need.

3. God Guides------

Dear Pastor(s) you can't lead, guide, or wait on anyone if you don't have a prayer, fasted life and relationship with Christ. People know if you live a fasted life.

ow? Glad you asked, Your MOUTH, ACTIONS, & BODY LANGUAGE will
XPOSE YOU! This will stop you from acting like a child. This will cause you
have side conversations with the church about your disagreements.

ead shepherds don't have feelings. Dead pastors have no opinions. Dead
hepherds think like Christ. Jesus was the greatest shepherd and he did not
etaliate against anyone. Pastors/shepherds/leaders if you don't walk in
umility, you will never lead or be respected by anyone but instead, you will
e talked about negatively by everyone. Grow up in **THE KINGDOM** leave
ehind the "church kingdom mindset"

Even though I walk through the darkest valley, I will fear no evil, for you are
ith me; your rod and your staff, they comfort me." (Psalm 23:4) God is
resent throughout all seasons of life, and thankfully even in those seasons
here we don't acknowledge His presence until later. This verse reminds us
hat we have no need to fear because the almighty God is for us, with, us, and
ill protect us. If we then consider ourselves as His sheep, and He our
hepherd, that is all the more reason not to fear. Realizing that God is not
ist our shepherd, but our good shepherd is news good enough to calm our
oubts, fears, and insecurities. Seeing God as our good shepherd means that
e recognize the deep love and care He has for us. His love is so deep that He
s guiding us throughout every season of our lives. He does not grow tired of
eing with us.

rue leaders have a clear vision for the future and live toward it.
eaders press beyond being SERVANT-LEADERS to becoming SHEPHERD-
EADERS.

EVENTS

"Go ahead & Live a little bit"

PINK BOSS BRUNCH

Saturday, September 30th

11am-2pm

Private Los Angeles Location

$50
Catered Brunch
Mimosas
Business
Music
Swag Bag

Jackie Johnson

THE BOSS MENTOR

Calling ALL FEMALE Entrepreneurs/Business Brands/ or Aspiring Business Owners! If you're ready to grow your business and take it to the next level. Don't miss this amazing networking event designed especially with you in mind!

Wear ANY shade of pink & bring your Boss Sisters/Besties with you!

WWW.THEBOSSMENTOR.ORG/EVENTS

January 12th thru 15th

NEXT STOP...
ARIZONA

PACKAGE INCLUDES

- ☑ EXCLUSIVE SWAG BAG
- ☑ EMPOWERMENT SESSIONS
- ☑ SESSION MATERIALS
- ☑ DAILY CATERED MEALS
- ☑ CANDLELIGHT DINNER
- ☑ GROUP ACTIVITIES

DEPOSIT REQUIRED TO REGISTER
FINAL PAYMENT DUE JULY 31ST

$600
PER PERSON

REGISTER NOW
WWW.P31WIVESCLUB.COM

ALABAMA

MARRIAGE ❤ & FAMILY
Therapist

JENNIFER MARION, MA MFTA

It's time to heal from past traumas and rid our lives, marriages, and families of the dysfunction and you won't have to do it alone

Book a session today!

SPIRIT OF LIFE & HOPE MINISTRIES

Weekly SERVICES

1ST MONDAY @6:30PM- Discipleship Training
TUESDAYS @4:30AM - Intecessory Prayer
THURSDAYS @7PM- Intecessory Prayer
THURSDAYS @7:30PM - Life Applications
1st & 3rd SUNDAYS @9am - Worship Service

More Information: (251) 287-5242
Email: info@solhministries.org

PASTOR
EARL MARION

ASSISTANT PASTOR
JENNIFER MARION

www.solhministries.org

ARKANSAS

INAMEINK

*PAINLESS TATTOOS OPTIONS

Tattoo artist

ARKANSAS LOCATION

BOOK & FOLLOW NOW

@INAMEINK

DOLLED BY DOLLY

Book Today!

Wig Creation
Wig Coloring
Wig Install
Tape-Ins
Ponytails
Sew-ins
Quickweaves
Braids & Locs
Natural Hair
Cut & Styling

CASH APP: $Dolly0128

Instagram: @dolly_rare

ARIZONA

WEEKLY MENU OPTIONS

Kingdom KITCHEN

EXPERIENCE A TASTE OF MISSISSIPPI
SOUL FOOD

*PRIVATE CATERING
*PERSONAL MEALS
*WEEKLY LUNCHES
*EVOLVING WEEKLY PUBLIC MENU

 TO ORDER CALL
602.731-0707

LOCAL DELIVERY AVAILABLE IN 85017 AREA: $5

EMAIL US: Kingdomkitchen01@gmail.com

KINGDOM 1ST HOME HEALTH CARE

OUR SERVICES

SERVICES ARE OFFERED TO ASSIST RESIDENTS WITH DAILY LIVING.

- One to three meals a day.

- Monitoring of medication.

- Personal care, dressing, bathing.

- Light Housekeeping and laundry.

- Social and recreational activities.

- Transportation to appointments

- Companionship

 (623) 306-9327

WE'RE HERE FOR YOU

IN HOME CARE

Provide care and/or assistance within the comfort of your own home.

RESPITE CARE

Planned or emergency care provided to your loved one when you need a helping hand

COMPANIONSHIP

Supporting a life of purpose and love.

**Email:
kingdom1sthome@gmail.com**

APPLY NOW

CALIFORNIA

KG BEAUTY   KG BEAUTY   KG BEAUTY

MY SERVICES *Los Angeles, CA*

BRAIDS

Singles (Natural Hair)
Box Braids

NATURAL HAIR

ash/Condition/Blow Out
t/Blow Out
lk Press
eratin

WEAVES

PONYTAIL
QUICK WEAVE
TRADITIONAL SEW IN
TAPE-INS

COLORING

LEACHING
LL COLOR
EACH & FULL COLOR

$25
ONSULTATION

SEND TO CASHAPP:
@kaylagirls

*NOT SURE WHAT YOU WANT OR HAVE QUESTIONS ABOUT SERVICES?
BOOK A CONSULTATION*

 @KAYG.BEAUTY_   www.thebossmentor.org/kayg-beauty

DOWNEY, CA

Because U Dessert It

CUSTOM SWEET TREATS
WORKSHOPS & GROUP CLASSES
FLORAL BOQUETS & ARRANGEMENTS

By Anayely

USE THE BELOW CODE
FOR A 10% DISCOUNT ON
DESSERT ORDERS

PINKDESSERT

FACEBOOK: @because_u_dessert_it
INSTAGRAM: @because_u_dessert_it

PINK MONEY LLC.

WELCOME
Pink Money
CUSTOMERS

CUSTOM APPAREL & GIFTS THAT INSPIRE, MOTIVATE, ENCOURAGE, & EMPOWER

  @pinkmoneyla

www.thebossmentor.org/pink-money

BUSINESS CARDS

The Boss Mentor

PRICE LIST

- $35 (100)/ $45 (250)/ $60 (500) STANDARD
- PREMIUM CARD STOCK- +7
- FREE PICKUP (BOYLE HEIGHTS)
- $6.99 SHIPPING
- 2-3 DAY TURNAROUND

WWW.THEBOSSMENTOR.ORG

THE BOSS MENTOR
BRAND

LEARN How To
Start Your T-shirt /Custom Print Business

Jackie Johnson
THE BOSS MENTOR

www.the boss mentor.org

Affordable Pricing

- Step by step instructions
- Virtual One on One Sessions
- Flexible training schedule
- Vendor lists for supplies
- Detail instructions on equipment
- Free Post training Support hours

$700

Manifested Truth Publishing

PUBLISH YOUR OWN BOOK

- Step by step instruction from established publisher and author
- Flexible session time
- Low cost printing
- Marketplace Selling
- Copyright
- ISBN purchase & imprint
- Post training support hours

www.the boss mentor.org/manifested-truth-publishing

GEORGIA

INDIANA

TRUE PROPHETIC UTTERANCE MINISTRIES

SUNDAYS
11AM

WORSHIP Service

SR. PASTOR: DR. DORVETTA PRICE

2051 N. EMERSON AVE., INDIANAPOLIS, IN 46218

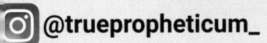 @truepropheticum_   www.tpuminsitries.wix.com/tpum

OHIO

FRIDAYS & SATURDAYS
SERVING THE COLUMBUS AREA

ORDER
(614) 638-8197
INSTAGRAM:
@dotsweekendfood

Delivery Available for Fee based on location

DOT'S WEEKEND DINNERS
SOUTHERN SOULFOOD

SIDES

Greens - $3.50
Mac & Cheese - $3.50
Baked Beans - $3.50

DINNERS

Barbeque Ribs: $16
Barbeque Quarters: $14
Fried Chicken: $12
Fish: $15
(Catfish or Talipia)

COMBOS

(4) Wings & Fries: $8
(10) Wings & Fies: $15

Dinners come with meat, 2 sides, slice of cake, and pop or bottle water

If you would like to advertise with us please follow instructions below! Next Deadline: September 1st for Holiday Issue!

Jackie Johnson
THE BOSS MENTOR

Grow your BUSINESS

ADVERTISE WITH US:

Cash App:
$TheBossCircle

Venmo:
fabfivejohnson@gmail.com

BOSS MY *Life* MAGAZINE

SUMMER FASHION TIPS

ROMANTIC HOT SPOTS

WHY CHOOSE US?

- ✓ OUR MAGAZINE IS BOTH LOCALLY OWNED AND MINORITY OWNED

- ✓ OUR LAST ISSUES WAS PURCHASED IN 8 U.S. STATES- WHICH MEANS THIS IS A OPPORTUNITY TO PRESENT YOUR BUSINESS, BRAND, OR EVENT OUTSIDE OF YOUR LOCAL COMMUNITY

- ✓ OUR AD PRICING IS AFFORDABLE INTENTIONALLY TO CREATE A NETWORK OF SUPPORT

Boss My Life Magazine is based out of Los Angeles, CA. The CEO & Editor in Chief is an amazing mom, entrepreneur, author, and vital part of the Boyle heights community. This magazine brings nothing but positivity and inspiration to every area of life from family, to spirituality, to business and education while highlighting great people that are on the rise to greatness.

BUSINESS CARD	QUARTER PAGE AD	HALF PAGE AD FULL PAGE AD
$15	$25	$50/$85

CONTACT US FOR MORE INFORMATION:

 thetcfirm@gmail.com   www.thebossmentor.org

MEET

OUR STAFF

EDITOR-IN-CHIEF
Jackie Johnson

FASHION WRITER
Mikel Kindell

FOOD & CULTURE
Tessa Swift

THERAPY HOUR
Jennifer Marion

BEAUTY-FUL
Kayla Kindell

FAMILY TIES
Eric & Latoria Curry

THE GOSPEL TRUTH
Dorvetta Price

If you'd like an opportunity to write for our magazine please contact us via our website: www.thebossmentor.org/contact-us or Email us at thetcfirm@gmail.com

Made in the USA
Las Vegas, NV
23 July 2023